The Integrity of Childhood

By
Kathy Charley

Copyright © MCMXCVII
by Kathy Charley

All rights reserved. No part of this book, either in part or in whole, may be reproduced, transmitted or utilized in any form or by any means, electronic, photographic or mechanical, including photocopying, recording, or by any information storage and retrieval system, without permission in writing from the author, except for brief quotations embodied in literary articles and reviews.

For permissions, or for adaptations, write the author at the address below.

International Standard Book Number: 0-942323-25-4

Author address:
Kathy Charley
1404 13th Ave. NW
Minot, North Dakota 58703

Published by
North American Heritage Press
Minot, North Dakota USA

Printed in the United States of America

Dedication

For all the children

This book is dedicated with love
to Sarah, Hattie and Zach,
who were my first teachers.

To Anne, Jane, Matthew, Luke, Meghan
and Sean who continue to inspire me
with their love and gentleness.

I love you very much.

Foreword

"Celebrate the Child in You" was the theme chosen for the fall conference of the North Dakota Association for the Education of Young Children. The idea our committee hoped to highlight was that if you are in touch with the child in you, you will better understand the child in front of you. Early childhood educators and caregivers need to be reminded from time to time that it's not so much what you teach the children that brings social, emotional, and cognitive growth as it is how you allow, understand, and truly value the hands-on way children naturally learn. Our committee was looking for presenters who shared this belief.

Then, one Sunday morning in July, I came downstairs to an infrequent husband-prepared breakfast. There were the usual lumps in his waffle batter, but there was an unusual lump in his throat as well. He had just read Kathy Charley's article in the *Minot Daily News*, "The Integrity of Childhood." He poured me a cup of coffee and insisted I sit right down and read. After reading two paragraphs I knew who our conference presenter must be. After reading the whole article, I knew that Kathy would have to do a slide show correlating her words with photographs of her children fingerpainting with pudding, building snowmen in the bathtub, and splashing in the puddles. (Some folks would have to see it to believe it.) And after seeing, believing, and responding to the presentation she shared with nearly 300 educators and childcare workers at our fall conference, I knew she had to "wrap her gift up" in book form and share it with people who need to know what her heart knows.

And what exactly does Kathy's heart know? — that childhood is a miraculous gift; that it is an "important, though not-so-sophisticated way of looking at the world;" that if we value children's needs to touch, crawl through, stir up, jump on, and examine things around them, we are giving them permission to follow natural curiosity down a wonder-filled path of learning. Imagine what it would be like to be a child in Kathy's care looking into her eyes and seeing acceptance and encouragement as you head toward the first puddle of spring. Imagine your very own mother, up to her ankles, sharing your "little celebration" of the new season. Imagine simply being yourself and realizing that somebody likes your ideas, your songs, your silly rhymes, your inventions, your experiments. In fact, somebody thinks you are a living, breathing wonder.

If you're standing in the book store wondering if you should take this book home, trust me, you should! If you are a parent, keep it for yourself as a reminder that childhood is a time in life worth revisiting. If you are a grandparent, give it to your children. If you are a teacher, especially of young children, read it regularly. If you are a person who believes in the integrity of childhood, take it home because it feels so good to read a book which shares your philosophy exactly.

Judy Winje
Mother of three
Grandmother of two
Director and Teacher of Escuela Preschool

Acknowledgements

I never really understood, nor paid much attention to acknowledgements at the beginning of a book until the dream of this book started to become a reality. It was then that I began to feel an overwhelming sense of gratitude to the people in my life whose example and inspiration have guided me throughout the task of writing this book. Without their support and encouragement, the words on these pages would remain tucked away in the back of my mind or scribbled on scraps of paper in a bottom drawer. To each of you…to all of you…my deepest respect and gratitude…

Judy Winje, who first encouraged me to share my thoughts.

Father Jim Starbuck, who taught me that my work is Holy.

Gary Thune, who inspired me with his gentle nudging and insistence that this message needed to be heard.

My mom and dad, who taught me to trust in God and believe in myself.

My husband Ralph, who in the midst of everything, continues to be "the wind beneath my wings."

And to God, the source of all my strength.

Introduction

Behind the pages of this book lies a deep conviction of the blessings and gifts that come to us through our children. Each child is born, delicate and innocent, ready to attain the full potential that is in God's design. Our privilege as parents is to gently and willingly allow each child to grow and become, as we give away a piece of our heart forever. Our children will give us a lifetime of memories. They will teach us valuable lessons…if we are humble enough to quiet ourselves…and listen.

This is a book about celebrating life with our children. It is about the importance of home and family and discovering the wonder inside of us all. It is about affirming our children while daring to experience the world through their little eyes. It is about celebrating each of us, as moms and dads…and each of our little ones as perfect creations and miraculous gifts from God.

I am fully convinced that the little lessons we learn from our children are the things that will remain. Our lives have been turned upside down since the birth of our children, and I thank God every day for (almost) all of it. God bless all of the children…always…and everywhere.

Kathy Charley

The Integrity Of Childhood

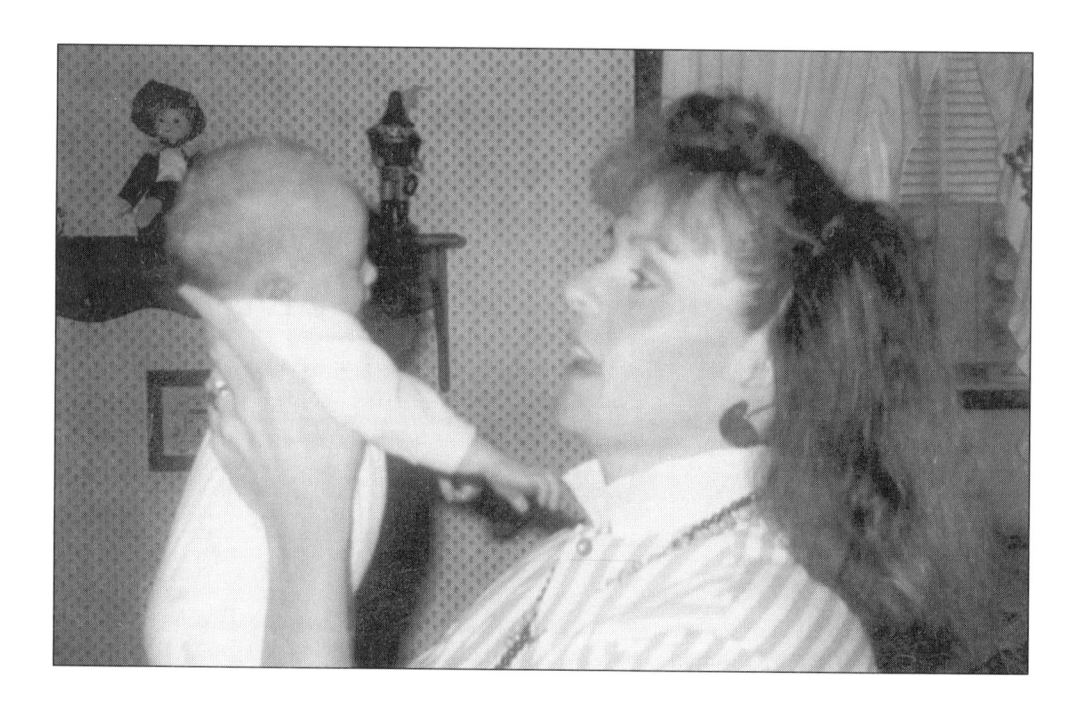

The Integrity Of Childhood

There are certain birthrights that you give up when you step into that mystical adventure called "motherhood": the right to a hot meal . . . the right to go to the bathroom alone . . . the promise to always crave macaroni and cheese at lunchtime and eat crusts of bread with a smile.

The Integrity Of Childhood

The Integrity Of Childhood

I haven't finished a thought or a sentence in months. I spend my days with God's littlest people and I have learned much from them.

I am an older-than-average mother of six younger-than-average children.

The Integrity Of Childhood

My life is one of diapers and play-dough, make-believe and purple dinosaurs. I carry a diaper bag instead of a purse, eat jello jigglers with my fingers and spend countless hours teaching my children how not to whine.

The Integrity Of Childhood

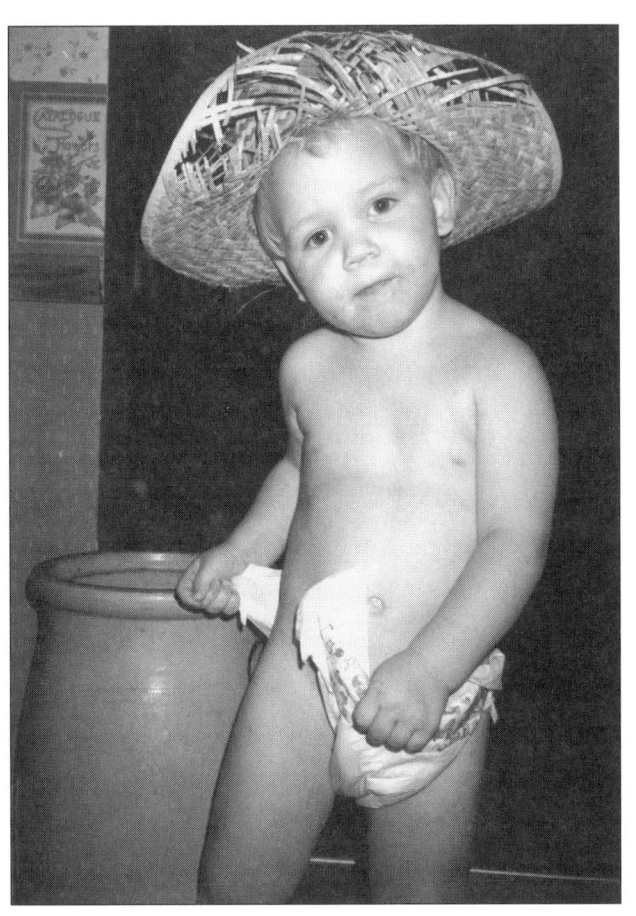

The Integrity Of Childhood

Barney is my friend and each morning I wait in line for my hug, so I can feel special, too.

The Integrity Of Childhood

I have only traveled through the beginning path of school and am miles from the growing pains of adolescence, where my real ability to understand will be challenged. I haven't had a lot of experience in game schedules and homework, school parties and carpools. But when people tell me "It'll get easier," I know they're not telling the truth.

The Integrity Of Childhood

So for now, I am grateful for this time I have, surrounded in a world of nursery rhymes and fingerpaint . . . lullabies . . . and potty training.

The Integrity Of Childhood

In the last few years, I've learned something very important. There is something miraculous about this gift called childhood. It is a whole new way of life.

The Integrity Of Childhood

It is an innocence. A wonder. A very important, though not-so-sophisticated way of looking at the world.

The Integrity Of Childhood

The Integrity Of Childhood

It is where many of life's most important lessons can be found.

The Integrity Of Childhood

The Integrity Of Childhood

The Integrity Of Childhood

There is a softness, a gentleness, that needs to be part of parenting. It is a privilege. It is God-given grace. There is much to learn in the short amount of time that we have these little ones. Perhaps we should let our children be the teachers.

The Integrity Of Childhood

Take a risk. Step out in faith with your children. Hold their hands and walk through the puddles with them.

Let there be times when chocolate pudding is for fingerpainting and popsicles for dripping in the sun.

The Integrity Of Childhood

The Integrity Of Childhood

Dance in the street when spring finally comes. Wake them up to see the full moon and forget about how tired they might be. Fill the bathtub with snow when it's too cold to play outside.

The Integrity Of Childhood

For at least a little while, let nothing else matter.

The Integrity Of Childhood

The Integrity Of Childhood

Why? Because we owe it to our children to let ourselves dream with them, to allow ourselves to be a child, so their little celebrations of life won't pass by unnoticed.

The Integrity Of Childhood

How else can we learn the lessons of childhood? How else can we come to expect the same miracles that they do? It's hard to do.

The Integrity Of Childhood

The Integrity Of Childhood

I believe in the integrity of childhood with every ounce of energy that is in me. And still, I want to slow down the clock, for there are many things I have to teach them, these little children.

The Integrity Of Childhood

They need to learn to sit quietly in church and not interrupt when I'm talking.

The Integrity Of Childhood

The Integrity Of Childhood

I want them to make their beds and chew with their mouths closed and please, not to go upstairs empty-handed.

The Integrity Of Childhood

Don't they realize what it costs to feed a family and that money doesn't grow on trees and for heaven's sake will someone PLEASE turn off the water in the bathroom?! The sink is going to overflow and we'll all slip on the floor and break our legs and I have no way of getting you to the emergency room because daddy is out of town and the fish will have NO WATER TO LIVE!! I have actually had this conversation with my children, though I'm certain it made no lasting impression. And in the quiet moments, I ask myself, "Why?"

The Integrity Of Childhood

The Integrity Of Childhood

I know why. There is a dream, a hope, that comes with parenting; that somehow, we can do it all, and have it all and be "effective" parents through it all.

The Integrity Of Childhood

But then, somewhere along the way, if we are lucky, we re-evaluate our priorities and realize that in spite of ourselves, and all of our tireless efforts, we can't do it all.

The Integrity Of Childhood

The Integrity Of Childhood

So we compromise. We sacrifice. We take some energy from here, and put it over there. It's all part of being a parent. And it's okay.

The Integrity Of Childhood

Sometimes I think we need to lighten up on ourselves, to not take ourselves so seriously, and let life be kinder to us. I remember the first time I proudly pushed our new double stroller through the zoo. I looked down and realized I had on two different sneakers. I was mortified. That was six years ago. Now I go to church meetings with gum stuck to the seat of my jeans and my turtleneck on inside out — and no one even notices. Or at least, I don't care — too much — if they do.

The Integrity Of Childhood

The Integrity Of Childhood

I want my children to be good just for the sake of being good.

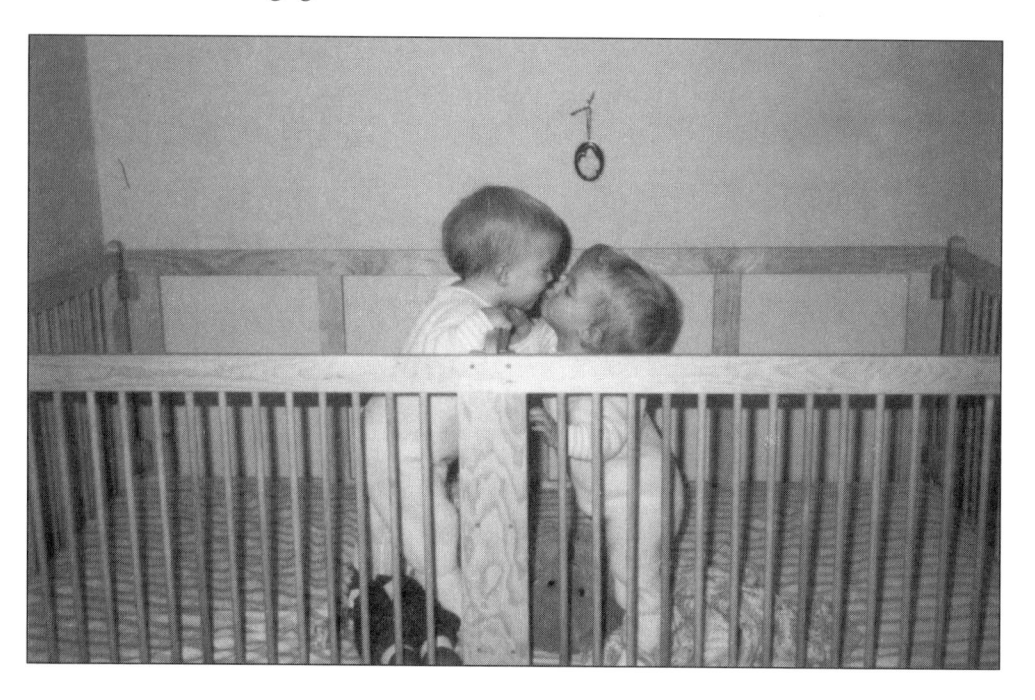

The Integrity Of Childhood

I want church to be meaningful and bedtime to be peaceful.

39

The Integrity Of Childhood

The Integrity Of Childhood

I want them to take baths in squeaky clean tubs with clear water and no germs, like you see in the magazines. I want our meals to be nutritious and well balanced, so we can become acquainted with the four food groups. But for some unknown reason, my vision and this reality have yet to meet.

The Integrity Of Childhood

So, I bribe my children when they have their pictures taken at Sears, and pray that at least some of them will fall asleep in church. We pile in and out of the tub: the boys, the girls, the babies, and hope that the hot water holds out and that no one dumps all the shampoo before the last one is finished.

The Integrity Of Childhood

43

The Integrity Of Childhood

The Integrity Of Childhood

I've introduced them all to the concept of brunch, in hopes of getting by with serving only one meal before the mad dash at noon for kindergarten. I pour generic Toasted O's into the Cheerios box, and try to pass it off as the real thing.

The Integrity Of Childhood

And we're still talking about menu planning. One of these days, it's bound to happen. I suppose, in the meantime, I'll continue frantically flipping through cookbooks at four o'clock and end up making the same old meatloaf.

The Integrity Of Childhood

But all of that is okay, for "this too, shall pass" . . . all too quickly, I'm afraid.

The Integrity Of Childhood

For now, I find comfort in the lessons my children have taught me: that socks and mittens don't have to match, what other people think isn't so very important, and no, they won't catch pneumonia from walking through puddles.

The Integrity Of Childhood

The Integrity Of Childhood

The Integrity Of Childhood

I've learned that sometimes diapers can go on backwards, milk does taste better with a straw, and they really do give up their pacifiers before the first day of kindergarten.

The Integrity Of Childhood

I believe in the importance of manners and family mealtime, reading and rocking, respect for yourself and others, and faith in God. I know that praying together, and pockets full of Cheerios can get you through almost anything.

The Integrity Of Childhood

I've also learned what's not important: wiping down woodwork . . . clean vans . . . popsicle drips on the kitchen floor . . . little finger smudges on windows . . . dust in the corner.

The Integrity Of Childhood

I know I can't stop the clock . . . and I know my heart will have to break many times before these children are grown. I remember how hard it was to let our daughters go to preschool. I didn't cry on the first day of school. I cried in the van on the way to open house, four months before school started.

The Integrity Of Childhood

It was hard, and I doubt that it will ever get any easier. But perhaps it will be somewhat less painful if I know I have spent these early years celebrating the importance of childhood with them.

The Integrity Of Childhood

With all of its creative chaos, there are many gifts our children give us each day.

The Integrity Of Childhood

Imagination . . .
   Creativity . . .
   Discovery . . .
   Patience.

57

The Integrity Of Childhood

We need to be there to receive them, one by one, with all the love and wonder with which they were given.

The Integrity Of Childhood

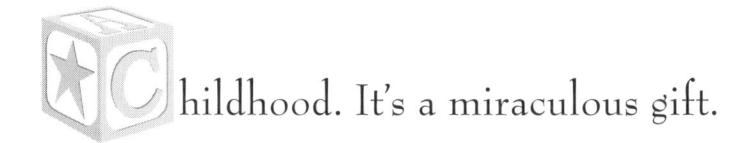

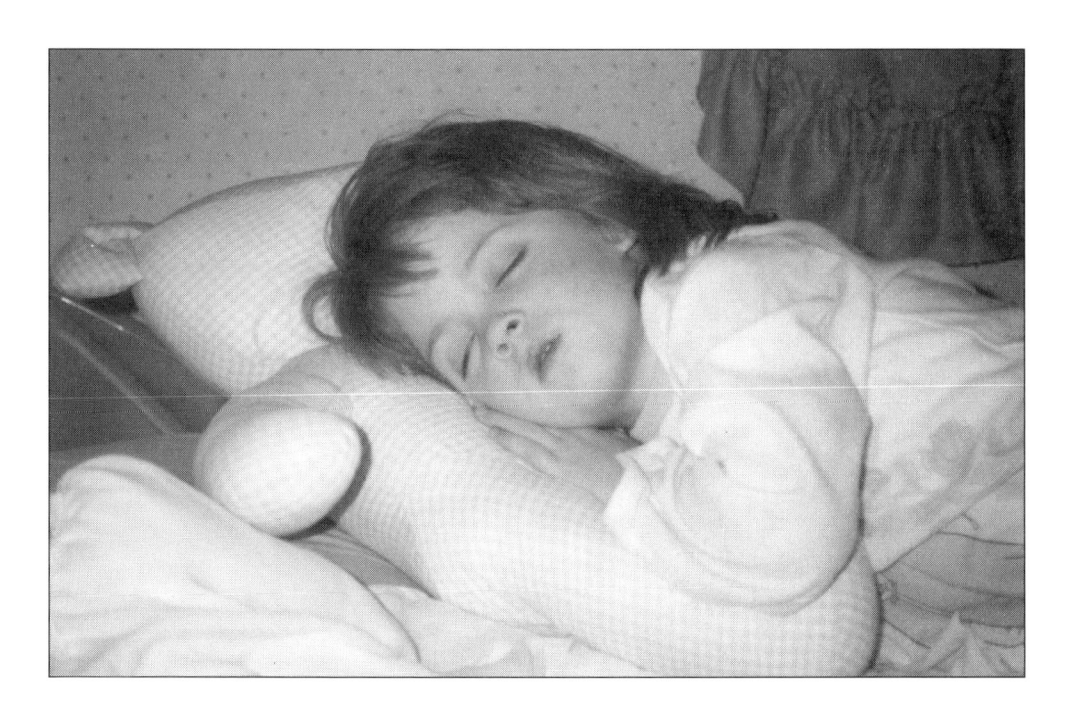

Childhood. It's a miraculous gift.

59